Alfred's Premier Piano Course

Dennis Alexander • Gayle Kowalchyk • E. L. Lancaster • Victoria McArthur • Martha Mier

Lesson 6 is available in two versions: Book with CD (#34643) or Book without CD (#33919).

Level 6 continues the steady development of artistry and keyboard skills that began in 1A and continued through 5.

- The keys of E-flat major, C and B minor (natural and harmonic) are introduced, as well as melodic minor scales, diminished triads, and major flat key signatures.
- Harmonic progressions include root position **V7** chords, the **ii–V7–I** chord progression, and diatonic triads.
- Mixed meter and syncopated rhythm patterns with eighth notes and sixteenth notes are used to create gradually more complex rhythm figures.
- Elements of music style in the Romantic and Contemporary periods introduce students to stylistic considerations in performing music of those eras, as well as to important keyboard composers.
- A special section on popular music traces the history and development of popular styles.
- Technical *Workouts* continue the development of skills, including two-octave scales beginning on black keys, two-octave arpeggios, note-against-note coordination, and more complex fingering principles.

Lesson Book 6 is designed to correlate with Theory and Performance Books 6 of *Alfred's Premier Piano Course*. When used together, they offer a fully integrated and unparalleled comprehensive approach to piano instruction. Level 6 is the last level of *Alfred's Premier Piano Course*.

The Book with CD version includes a recording that provides a *performance* model and *practice* companion. Each title is performed twice on acoustic piano—a *performance* tempo and a slower *practice* tempo. See page 57 for information on the CD.

Edited by Morton Manus

Cover Design by Ted Engelbart
Interior Design by Tom Gerou
Illustrations by Jimmy Holder
Music Engraving by Linda Lusk

ISBN-13: 978-0-7390-6488-7 Book only
ISBN-13: 978-0-7390-6876-2 Book & CD

Contents

Premier Music Review 2
Mixed Meter. 6
New Italian Term—*espressivo* 6
Diminished Triads 8
B Minor Scale. 9
New Italian Term—*rallentando*. 10
E♭ Major Scale 12
The Primary Chords in E♭ Major 12
Three Types of Minor Scales 14
C Minor Scale. 15
New Italian Term—*robusto*. 16
The Primary Chords in C Harmonic Minor 17
Musical Style Periods: The Romantic Period. . . . 18
New Italian Term—*subito* 19
Flat Key Signatures 22
Two-Octave Scales Beginning on Black Keys . . . 23
New Italian Term—*loco* 25
New Italian Term—*calore* 26
The Primary Chords in D♭ Major. 27
Musical Style Periods: The Contemporary Period . 28
New Italian Term—*presto* 28
Diatonic Triads 30
Chord Progressions 31
Root Position **V7** Chords 34
The **ii–V7–I** Chord Progression 34
Musical Style Periods: Popular Music. 40
New Italian Terms—*misterioso, animato* 44
New Italian Term—*lento maestoso* 54

2

Premier Music Review

1. Write the counts (by measure) under the notes—then tap and count aloud.

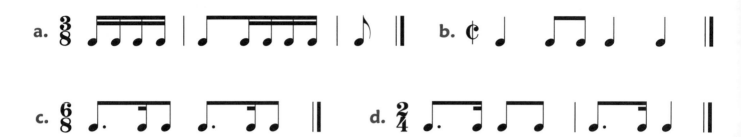

2. Draw a line from the term or name on the left to its matching definition on the right.

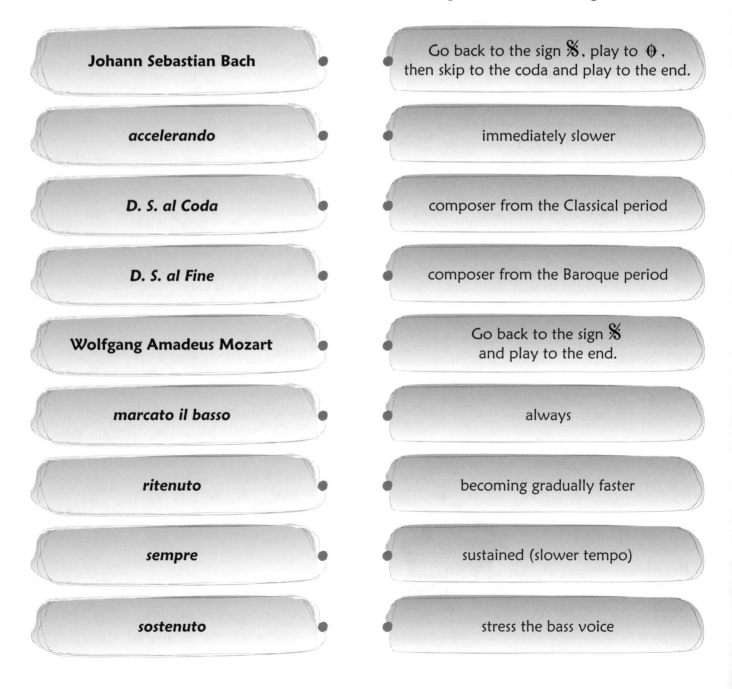

Johann Sebastian Bach	Go back to the sign 𝄋, play to ⊕, then skip to the coda and play to the end.
accelerando	immediately slower
D. S. al Coda	composer from the Classical period
D. S. al Fine	composer from the Baroque period
Wolfgang Amadeus Mozart	Go back to the sign 𝄋 and play to the end.
marcato il basso	always
ritenuto	becoming gradually faster
sempre	sustained (slower tempo)
sostenuto	stress the bass voice

3. Complete the scales by writing the missing notes. Use half notes, and sharps and flats if needed.

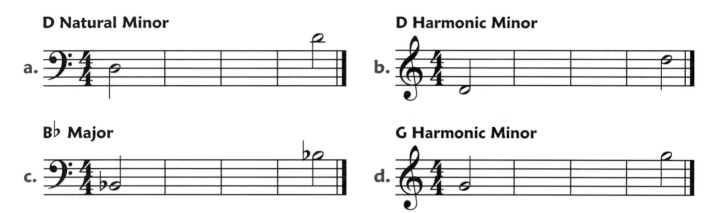

D Natural Minor

a.

D Harmonic Minor

b.

B♭ Major

c.

G Harmonic Minor

d.

4. Complete the sharp key signatures.

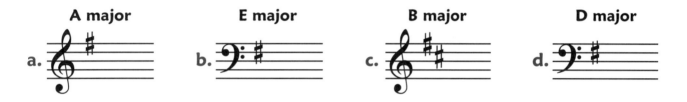

A major

a.

E major

b.

B major

c.

D major

d.

5. *Raise* the top note of each major triad one half step to write an augmented triad. Then play.

a.   b.   c.   d.

6. Circle the name of each triad. Then play.

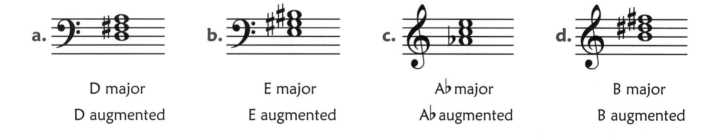

a.   b.   c.   d.

D major   E major   A♭ major   B major

D augmented   E augmented   A♭ augmented   B augmented

7. **True or False**

   a. An *ostinato* is a short musical pattern that repeats once.   true   false   (circle one)

   b. *Vivace* means "lively tempo, faster than *allegro*."   true   false   (circle one)

Scherzo

CD 1/2 GM 1

Carl Maria von Weber (1786–1826) was a German composer born into a family with no links to nobility, although the name "von" implies otherwise. Weber was mostly known as an opera composer, but he had many famous pianists among his fans, including Franz Liszt.

Carl Maria von Weber

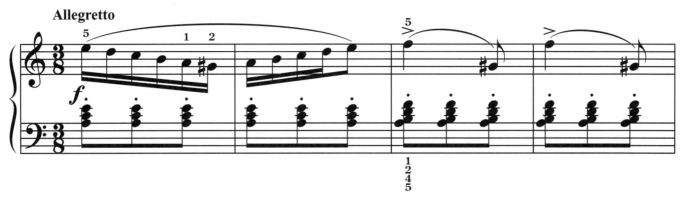

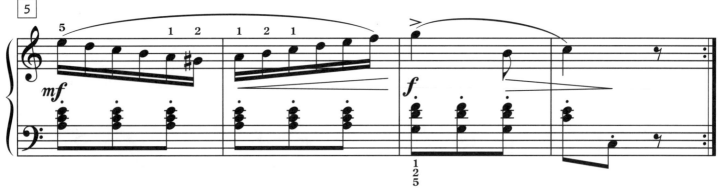

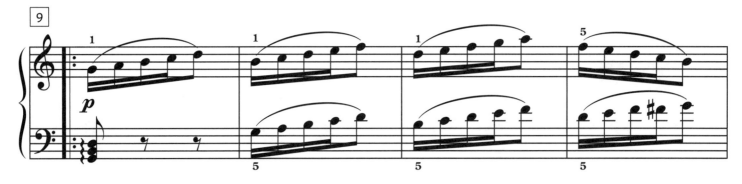

Rhythm Workout **Mixed Meter**

When 2 or more time signatures occur within a piece, the piece is considered to be in *mixed meter*. On your lap, tap the rhythm 3 times daily as you count aloud. Keep the eighth notes equal.

Black Is the Color
(of My True Love's Hair)

CD 3/4 GM 2

Appalachian Folk Song

Moderately slow, with freedom

mp *espressivo* (with expression)

Diminished Triads

Theory Book: page 5
Performance Book: pages 8–9

The word *diminish* means *to make smaller.*

A minor triad becomes diminished when the 5th is lowered
one half step. A small circle (°) indicates a diminished chord.

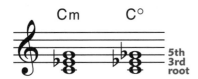

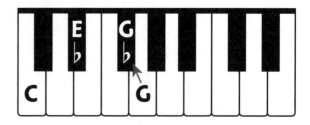

To make a C minor triad diminished, lower G (the 5th) one half step to G♭.

Playing Minor and Diminished Triads

Play *minor* and *diminished* triads. Lower the top note of the *minor* triad one
half step to form a *diminished* (°) triad. Practice one group of triads each day.

Group 1: Cm, Gm, Fm (**Minor Triads:** white key–black key–white key)

- Transpose to Gm and Fm.
- Play one octave lower with the LH.

Group 2: Dm, Am, Em (**Minor Triads:** white key–white key–white key)

- Transpose to Am and Em.
- Play one octave lower with the LH.

Group 3: C♯m, G♯m, D♯m (**Minor Triads:** different white-key and black-key patterns)

- Transpose to G♯m and D♯m.
- Play one octave lower with the LH.

Group 4: B♭m, Bm, F♯m (**Minor Triads:** different white-key and black-key patterns)

- Transpose to Bm and F♯m.
- Play one octave lower with the LH.

B Minor Scale
Relative Minor of D Major

The *relative minor* scale begins on the 6th note of the major scale. Therefore, B minor is the *relative minor* of D major. The keys of D major and B minor have two sharps in the key signature—F♯ and C♯.

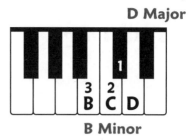

D Major

B Minor

You can also find the relative minor by counting 3 half steps *down* from the tonic.

B Natural Minor Scale

In the B natural minor scale, there are two sharps (F♯–C♯).

Half steps occur between notes 2–3 (C♯–D) and 5–6 (F♯–G).

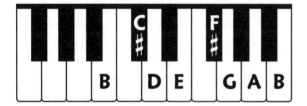

B Harmonic Minor Scale

The B harmonic minor scale is the same as the B natural minor scale, but with the 7th (A) raised a half step. The A♯ is written as an accidental.

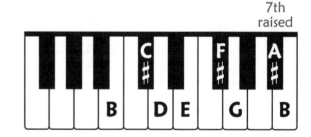

Playing the B Natural and Harmonic Minor Scale—Hands Separately

Say the finger numbers as you practice slowly. Play the LH 2 octaves *lower* than written. Memorize the fingering.

B Natural Minor

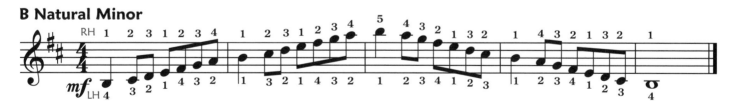

B Harmonic Minor

Theory Book: page 7
Performance Book: pages 10–11

New Italian Term

rallentando (rall.) =
becoming gradually slower

Playing with Expressive Tone

Tolling Bells paints a tone picture of large ringing bells in a church steeple.

● Circle the long rhythmic value notes in measures 1–7 and 17–24. These notes and the octaves in measures 25–28 represent the bell tones.

● Play each of the bell tones with relaxed *arm weight*.

● Listen for a ringing bell tone for these important notes!

Tolling Bells

CD 5/6   GM 3

Stephen Heller (1815–1888)
Op. 125, No. 8

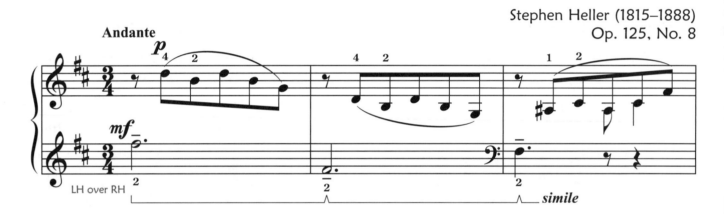

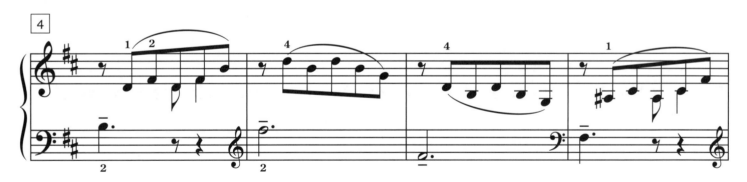

Closer Look *Circle the broken diminished chords in the LH of measures 9 and 13.*

E♭ Major Scale

The E♭ major scale contains 8 notes—
the E♭ 5-finger pattern + 3 notes.

Half steps occur between notes 3–4 (G–A♭)
and 7–8 (D–E♭).

In the E♭ major scale, there are three flats—
B♭, E♭, and A♭.

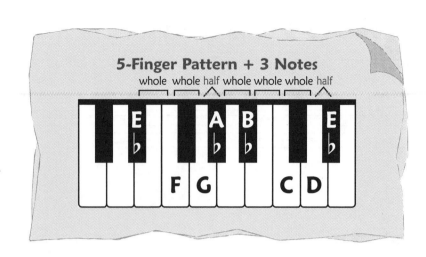

Playing the E♭ Major Scale—Hands Separately

Say the finger numbers as you practice slowly. Memorize the fingering.

Right Hand

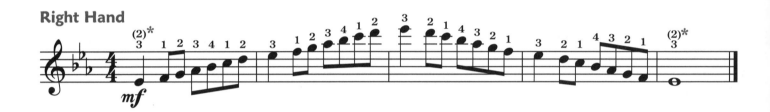

Left Hand

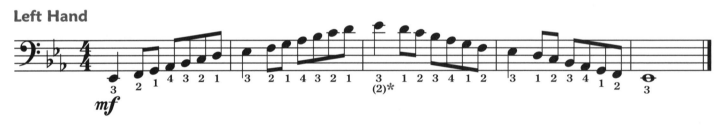

* Many pianists prefer to begin and end the RH scale with finger 2 and
play the highest note of the LH scale with finger 2 before descending.

The Primary Chords in E♭ Major

Play **I**, **IV** and **V⁷**, saying the chords names aloud.

Somethin' Blue

Theory Book: page 9
Performance Book: page 12

CD 7/8 GM 4

Three Types of Minor Scales

There are 3 types of minor scales: *natural*, *harmonic*, and *melodic*.

1. **Natural minor scale**—uses *only* the notes of the relative major scale. The **A natural minor scale** uses the notes of the C major scale.

2. **Harmonic minor scale**—same as the *natural minor scale* but raises the 7th note a half step. The **A harmonic minor scale** raises the 7th note (G) a half step to G♯.

3. **Melodic minor scale**—same as the *natural minor scale* but raises the 6th and 7th notes a half step going *up*, and returns to the natural minor going *down*. The **A melodic minor scale** raises the 6th (F) and 7th (G) notes a half step to F♯ and G♯ going *up*; they become F♮ and G♮ going *down*.

Playing Melodic Minor Scales—Hands Separately

Play the LH 2 octaves *lower* than written. Memorize the fingering.

A Melodic Minor

E Melodic Minor

B Melodic Minor

D Melodic Minor

G Melodic Minor

C Minor Scale

Relative Minor of E♭ Major

The *relative minor* scale begins on the 6th note of the major scale. Therefore, C minor is the *relative minor* of E♭ major. The keys of E♭ major and C minor have three flats in the key signature—B♭, E♭ and A♭.

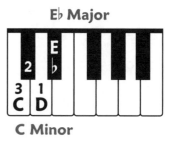

E♭ Major / C Minor

You can also find the relative minor by counting 3 half steps *down* from the tonic.

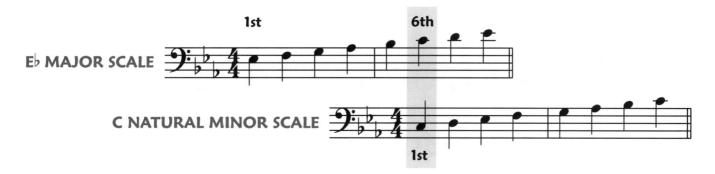

E♭ MAJOR SCALE — C NATURAL MINOR SCALE

C Harmonic Minor Scale

The C harmonic minor scale is the same as the C natural minor scale, but with the 7th (B♭) raised a half step to B♮. The B♮ is written as an accidental.

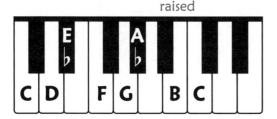

C Melodic Minor Scale

The C melodic minor scale is the same as the C natural minor scale, but raises the 6th (A♭) and 7th (B♭) notes a half step to A♮ and B♮ going *up*; they become A♭ and B♭ going *down*.

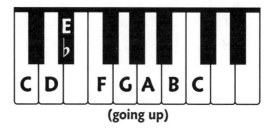

(going up)

Playing the C Minor Scales—Hands Separately

Say the finger numbers as you practice slowly. Play the LH 2 octaves *lower* than written. Memorize the fingering.

Natural Minor

- Play again, raising the 7th (B-flat to B-natural) for the C harmonic minor scale.

Melodic Minor

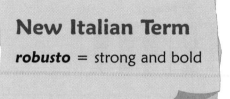

New Italian Term

robusto = strong and bold

Workout 1 2-Octave Arpeggios

Play each 2-octave arpeggio *legato*. Keep the arm relaxed and fluid as you glide up the keyboard.
Play 3 times each day.

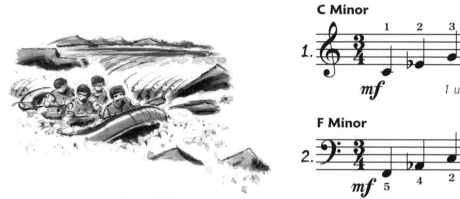

Shooting the Rapids

CD 9/10 GM 5

Premier Performer *Play the eighth-note triplets evenly, observing the crescendo without accenting individual notes.*

The Primary Chords in C Harmonic Minor

Play **i**, **iv** and **V⁷**, saying the chords names aloud.
Remember that the **i** and **iv** chords are minor.

2nd time RH 8va

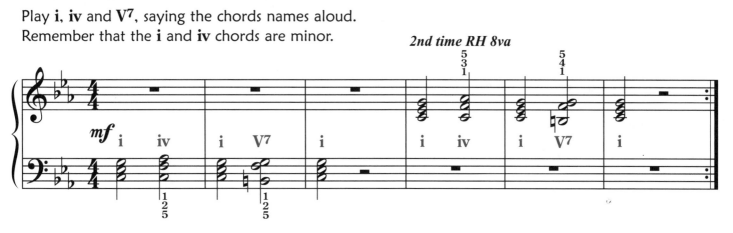

Musical Style Periods: The Romantic Period (1820–1900)

Music from the Romantic period often represents strong emotions but not necessarily those relating to "romance" or "love." Composers wrote pieces that demonstrated many moods, such as dramatic and stormy, thoughtful and dreamy, or inspiring and uplifting. Romantic music was intended to communicate personally with the listener.

During the Romantic Period:

✔ Short character pieces for piano became popular, yet older forms such as sonatas became longer.

✔ The modern piano reached the height of its development, paving the way for famous concert pianists like Franz Liszt and Clara Schumann. Their popularity rivaled the pop stars of today!

✔ Three important keyboard composers were Frédéric Chopin (1810–1849), Edvard Grieg (1843–1907), and Robert Schumann (1810–1856).

1839 Frédéric Chopin completed his *Preludes*, Op. 28, for piano.

1848 Robert Schumann composed *Album for the Young*, Op. 68, for piano.

1876 Alexander Graham Bell invented the telephone.

1880 Thomas Edison invented the light bulb.

Sight-Reading

Play these melodies from the Romantic period.
Count aloud.

1. Waltz in A Minor

Frédéric Chopin
Op. Posthumous

2. The Happy Farmer (from *Album for the Young*)

Robert Schumann
Op. 68, No. 10

Frisch und munter (Brisk and merry)

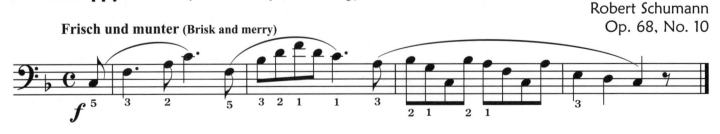

Spinning Song

CD 11/12 GM 6

Theory Book: page 14
Performance Book: pages 18–19

Albert Ellmenreich (1816–1905)
Op. 14, No. 4

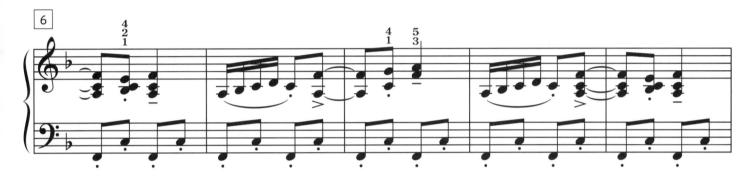
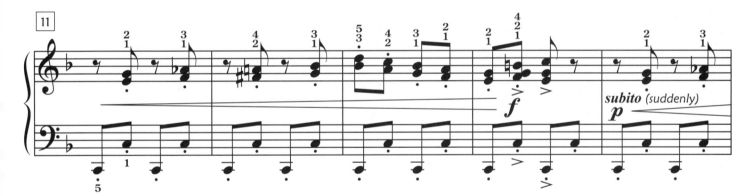
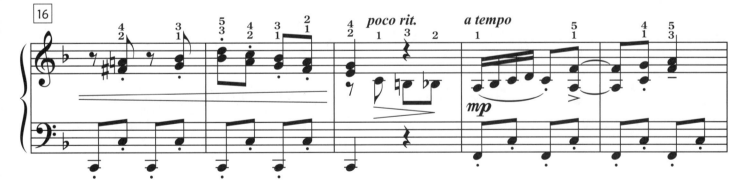
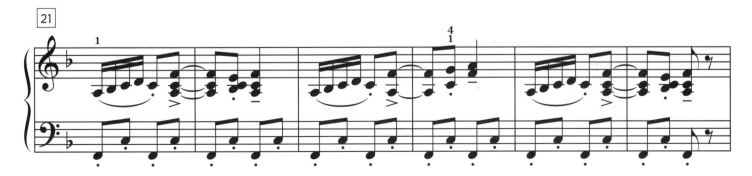

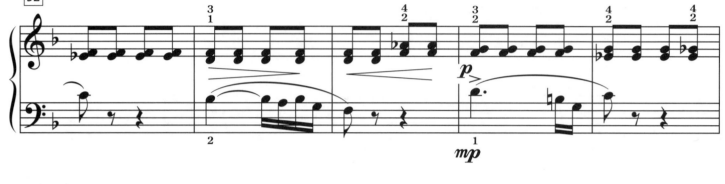

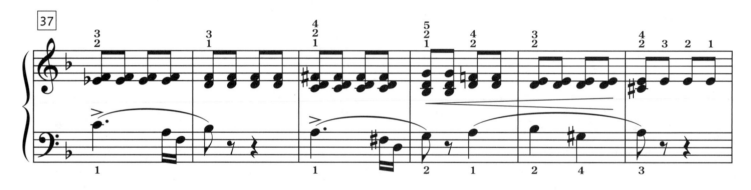

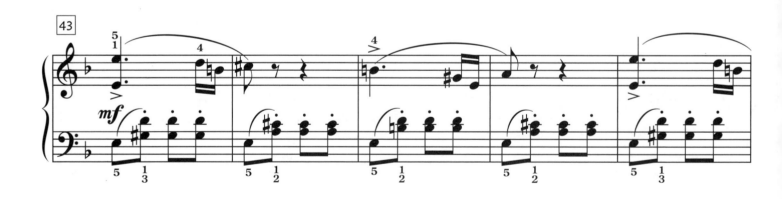

Flat Key Signatures

The key signature (the sharps or flats at the beginning of the staff) identifies two things:

- The *key* of the piece.
- The *sharps* or *flats* to be played throughout the piece.

The flats that are used in key signatures are *always* written in the same order on the staff: B E A D G C F

Play the flats in order on the keyboard.

B E A D G C F

Memorize the order of the flats. The order of flats in a key signature is the reverse of the order of sharps. To help you remember:

BEAD Goes **C**enter **F**ront.

Finding a Flat Key Signature's Name
(for keys with more than one flat)

Find the next to last flat.

This is the name of the major key.

Next to the last flat: B♭

Key of B♭ Major

You have already learned the following flat key signatures:

- F major—1 flat
- B♭ major—2 flats
- E♭ major—3 flats

Circle the next to the last flat, then name the key.

Key of ____ major

Key of ____ major

Key of ____ major

Two-Octave Scales Beginning on Black Keys

In this level and in previous levels you have played B♭ (2 flats) and E♭ (3 flats) major scales. Follow the fingering below and play the scales hands separately for two octaves.

	1st octave	2nd octave			1st octave	2nd octave
	(2)*				(2)	
B♭ RH:	4 1 2 3 1 2 3	4 1 2 3 1 2 3 4		**E♭** RH:	3 1 2 3 4 1 2	3 1 2 3 4 1 2 3
LH:	3 2 1 4 3 2 1	3 2 1 4 3 2 1 3		LH:	3 2 1 4 3 2 1	3 2 1 4 3 2 1 3
		(2)				(2)

*Alternate fingering

New Flat-Key Major Scales Beginning on Black Keys

Name the flats in each key and circle each note that is played as a flat.
Then practice hands separately. Play the LH two octaves *lower* than written.

Key of A♭ Major
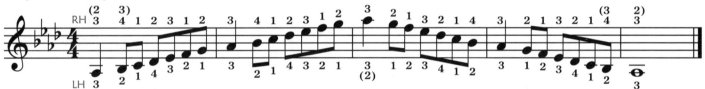

Key of D♭ Major

Key of G♭ Major

Hints for remembering the fingering of two-octave major scales that begin on black keys:
- The scales of B♭, E♭, A♭, and D♭ use the same fingering in the LH.
- Finger 4 in the RH can always play B♭.

Rhythm Workout

On your lap, tap the rhythm 3 times daily as you count aloud. Keep the eighth notes equal throughout.

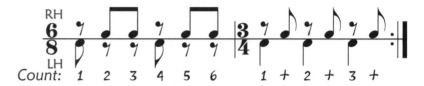

Toccata ritmico*

CD 13/14 GM 7

* *Ritmico is an Italian term meaning rhythmic.*

A **nocturne** (night song) is a quiet, lyrical romantic piece usually written for piano. It often has an expressive melody over a broken-chord accompaniment. John Field (1782–1837), an Irishman, was the first composer to write nocturnes. Frédéric Chopin's (1810–1849) 21 nocturnes are considered masterpieces.

Workout 2 LH Cross-Overs

Play 3 times each day.

Nocturne in ___* Major

CD 15/16 GM 7

New Italian Term

calore = with warmth

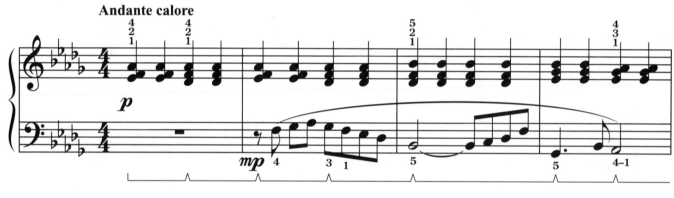

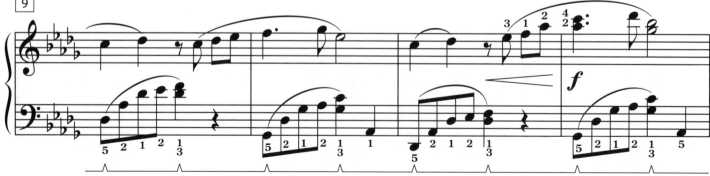

* Look at the key signature and name the key.

Premier Performer — *Bring out the singing melody as it moves from LH to RH.*

The Primary Chords in D♭ Major

Play **I**, **IV** and **V⁷**, saying the chords names aloud.

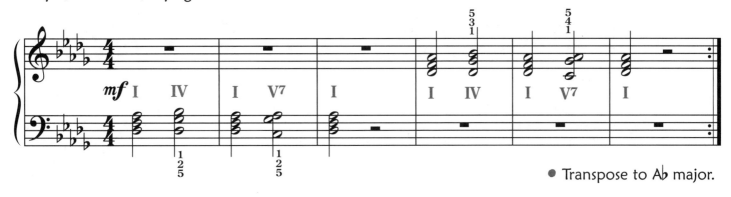

● Transpose to A♭ major.

Musical Style Periods: The Contemporary Period (1900–present day)

Contemporary means *something that is current.* Future music historians will probably divide the Contemporary period into at least two separate periods, but for now, all serious music written since 1900 is considered to be "contemporary." Sometimes this period is also called *Modern* or *20th Century.*

During the Contemporary Period:

✔ Many different and interesting sounds, some not very melodic and even "clashing," are characteristics of some composers' styles.

✔ The piano continues its popularity. Since the 1970s and through today, electronic or digital pianos have become common. These pianos often have optional "non-piano" sounds, as well as recording features.

✔ Three important keyboard composers were Béla Bartók (1881–1945), Claude Debussy (1862–1918), and Sergei Prokofiev (1891–1953). Sometimes Claude Debussy is called an *Impressionist,* a special category of Contemporary music written mainly in France.

1910 Béla Bartók wrote the *Romanian Folk Dances* for piano.

1936 Sergei Prokofiev completed *Peter and the Wolf* for orchestra and narrator.

1969 Apollo 11 successfully achieved the first manned moon landing.

1973 The invention of the Internet changed communication and information-exchange forever.

Sight-Reading

Play this melody from the Contemporary period. Count aloud.

Bagatelle, Op. 5, No. 10   Alexander Tcherepnin

Brâul*

(Romanian Folk Dances)

CD 17/18 GM 9

Béla Bartók (1881–1945)
Sz. 56, No. 2

Rhythm Workout

On your lap, tap the rhythm 3 times daily.
Notice the 5 sixteenth notes played in the
same time as 4 sixteenth notes.

Pedal is optional.

2nd time poco rit.

* A *brâul* was originally a chain dance for men. The men sometimes held on
to each other's belt, but holding on to the shoulders is more common today.

Diatonic Triads

Triads may be built on any note of any scale using the sharps or
flats in the key signature. They are labeled with Roman numerals.
These triads are called *diatonic triads*.

Major Keys

The *diatonic triads* in any major key consist of *major*, *minor*, and *diminished*
(5th is lowered one half step) chords. Play triads of the key in C major.

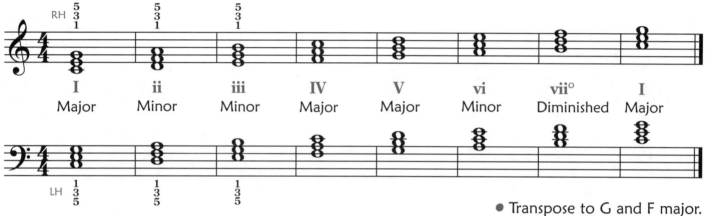

• Transpose to G and F major.
Use the sharps or flats in the key signature.

Harmonic Minor Keys

The *diatonic triads* in any harmonic minor key consist of *major*, *minor*, *diminished*, and
augmented (5th is raised one half step) chords. Play triads of the key in A harmonic minor.

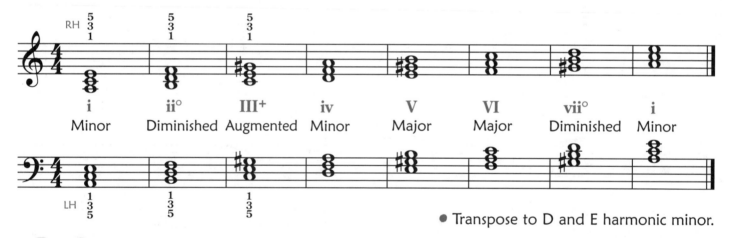

• Transpose to D and E harmonic minor.

Sight-Reading

Play this excerpt from the Contemporary period. The RH uses white-key
diatonic triads. The LH plays black keys (except for the last note).

O Polichinelo (from *The Baby's Family*)

Heitor Villa-Lobos

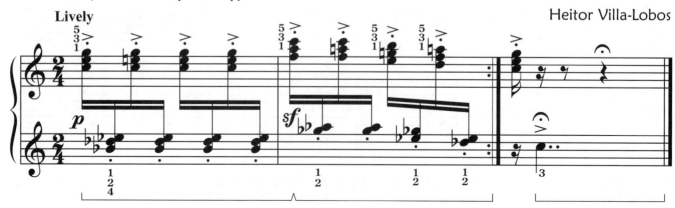

Chord Progressions

A chord progression is a series of chords, moving from one to another.
The *Canon in D* by Johann Pachelbel is based on a chord progression
that uses triads of the key of D major in the following order.

Practice the "Pachelbel chord progression" hands separately, then hands together.

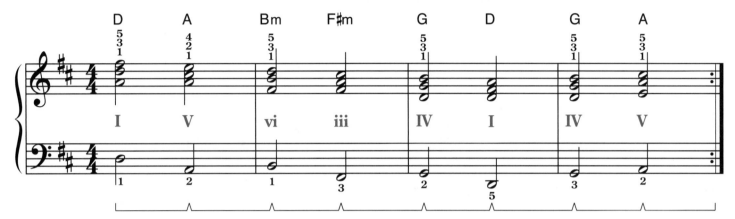

> **Johann Pachelbel** (1653–1706) was a German composer, organist, and teacher. Although Pachelbel was well known during his lifetime, today he is known almost exclusively for one piece, Canon in D, recognizable by most people through its appearance in movies, TV programs, and commercials.

Canon in D

CD 19/20 GM 10

Johann Pachelbel
(adapted)

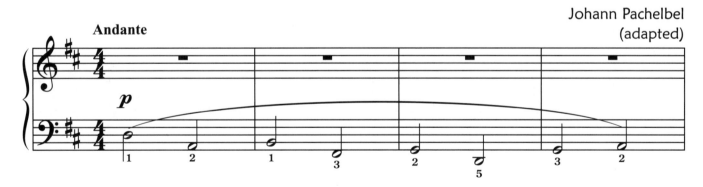

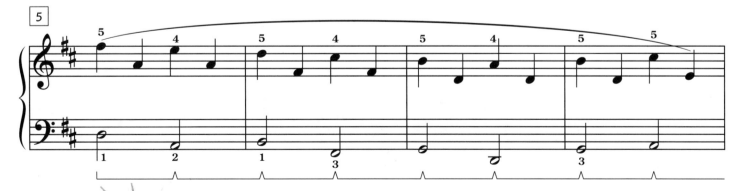

🌟 *Premier Performer* To help establish a good tempo, think about the melody in measure 25 before you begin.

Root Position V⁷ Chords

The **V⁷** chord is built on the 5th note of the scale.
The **V⁷** chord in C major has 4 notes: G B D F.

Play **V⁷** and **I**, saying the chord names aloud.
The 3rd or 5th of the **V⁷** chord is often omitted when played in root position.

Key of C Major

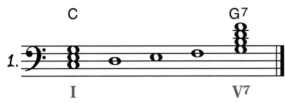

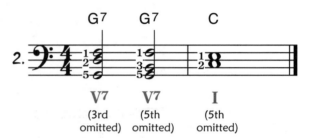

The **V⁷** chord in C minor has 4 notes: G B D F. The B-natural is used to build the **V⁷** chord based on the harmonic minor scale.

Key of C Minor

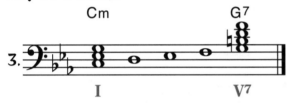

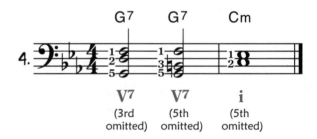

The ii–V⁷–I Chord Progression

The **ii–V⁷–I** chord progression occurs frequently in both classical and popular music.
In this progression, the **ii** chord is often played in first inversion.

Key of C Major

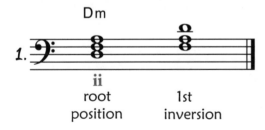

Play **ii–V⁷–I**, saying the chord names aloud.

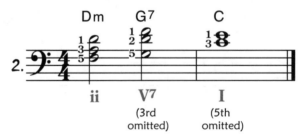

Key of C Minor

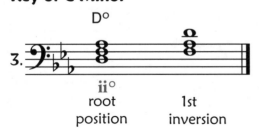

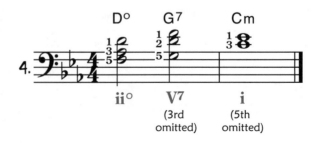

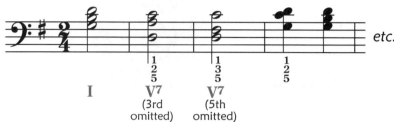

Workout 3 Blocking

Block (play at the same time) all 3 notes
of the LH chords in measures 1–7.

Écossaise*

CD 21/22 GM 11

Ludwig van Beethoven
(1770–1827)

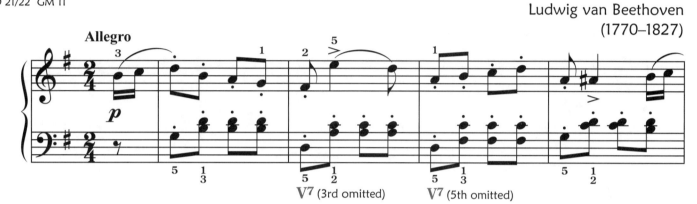

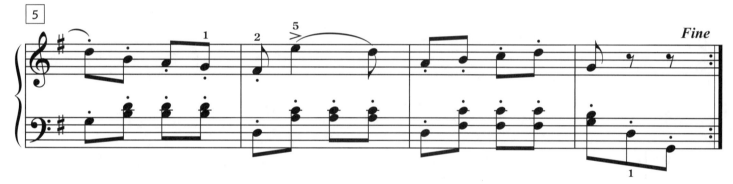

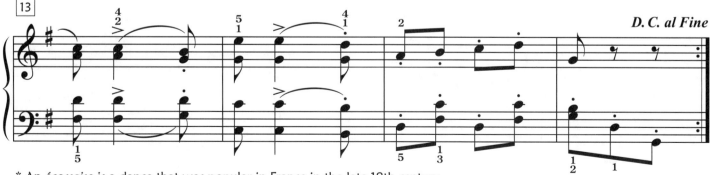

* An *écossaise* is a dance that was popular in France in the late 18th century.
Some historians believe that it is the French interpretation of a dance from Scotland.

Jazz Cafe

CD 23/24 GM 12

Workout 4 **LH Moves**

Play 3 times each day.

Bagatelle

CD 25/26 GM 13

Anton Diabelli (1781–1858)
Op. 125, No. 10

ii
(1st inversion)

V7

I

Musical Style Periods: Popular Music

Popular music is music that is not "serious" or classical in style. It is considered different from classical music since it has more immediate wide appeal but often for a shorter period of time. Popular music had its beginnings in the later part of the 19th century and has evolved since that time.

Popular Music:

✔ Is very diverse in style and includes ragtime, jazz, rock, country, folk, rap, hip-hop, gospel, and Broadway.

✔ Can be music for casual singing or dancing. Huge stadiums sometimes are filled for concerts by top popular music artists.

✔ Is sometimes short-lived in popularity, meaning that a pop artist or song can be a hit one day, then almost forgotten a few months later.

1895 Tin Pan Alley began when several music publishers set up offices in the same district of New York City. Leading Tin Pan Alley composers were Irving Berlin, George Gershwin, and Cole Porter.

1965 Over 55,000 fans packed New York City's Shea Stadium to hear a concert by the British rock group The Beatles.

1974 The Academy award-winning movie *The Sting* re-established the popularity of Scott Joplin's (1867–1917) ragtime music. *The Entertainer* is one of the biggest hits from the movie.

2002 The TV program American Idol made its debut. Since that time, it has launched careers for many recording stars and has entertained millions of viewers.

Sight-Reading

Play this popular melody. Although it was written in 1941, President Barack Obama and First Lady Michelle Obama used this song for their first dance at the Presidential Inaugural Balls in 2009.

At Last

Music by Harry Warren
Lyrics by Mack Gordon

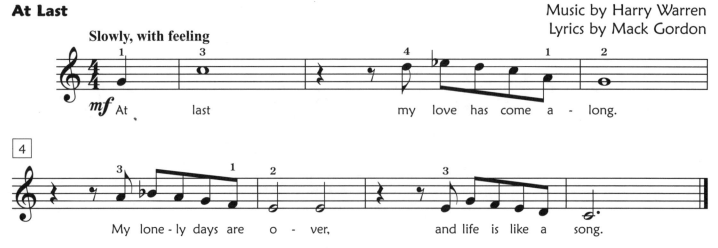

At last my love has come a - long.
My lone - ly days are o - ver, and life is like a song.

Chattanooga Choo Choo

Chattanooga Choo Choo *was one of the most popular songs in the big-band Swing Era. In 1941, the Glenn Miller recording became the first to be certified as a Gold Record, with sales of 1.2 million copies. The inspiration for the song was said to be a small, wood-burning steam locomotive, now on exhibit at the former Terminal Station in Chattanooga, Tennessee.*

CD 27/28 GM 14

Music by Harry Warren
Lyrics by Mack Gordon

Practice Plan

Section A (measures 1–30 and measures 57–86)

1. Practice each hand separately, listening for the crisp *staccato* notes in measures 1–26 and 57–82.

2. On your lap, tap the rhythm of measures 3–4 hands together. Then play, hands together.

Section B (measures 31–56)

1. Practice each hand separately, listening for the *legato* phrasing in RH.

2. Silently "play" the LH chords as you play the singing RH melody.

Coda (measures 87–96)

1. Practice measures 87–91 slowly, listening that the hands always play exactly together.

2. Silently practice the moves to the different octaves in measures 92–95.

New Italian Terms

misterioso = mysteriously
animato = animated, lively

Ballade*

CD 29/30 GM 15

Johann Burgmüller
(1806–1874)

Section A

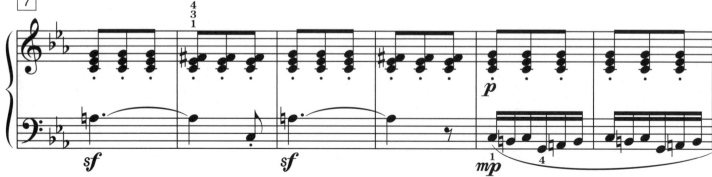

* A *ballade* is a piece that tells a dramatic story.

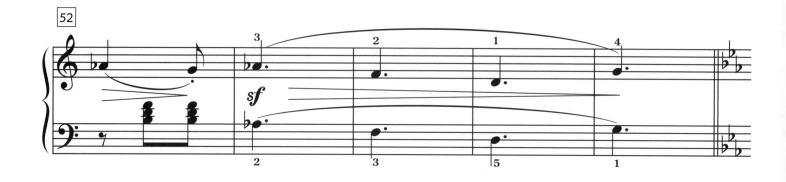

Section A

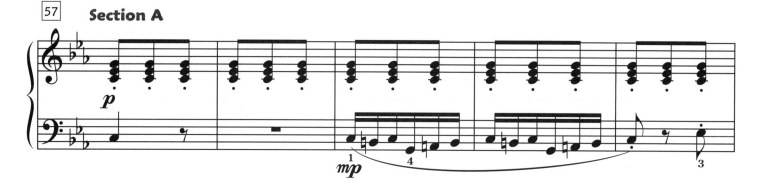

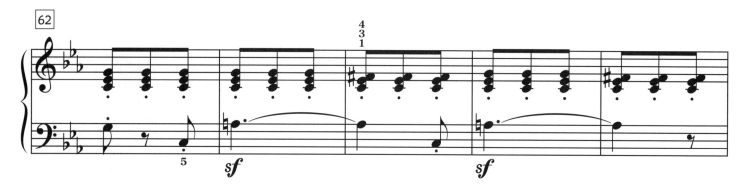

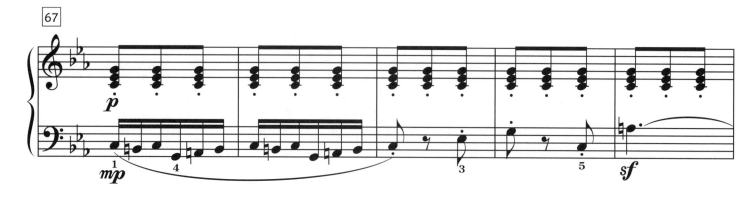

Theory Book: page 30
Performance Book: pages 36–37

Workout 5 Finger Substitution

Play 3 times each day.

Sicilienne*

CD 31/32 GM 16

Johann Sebastian Bach (1685–1750)
(adapted)

* A *sicilienne* is a 17th- and 18th-century dance of Sicilian (a region in southern Italy) origin.
  This *Sicilienne* is adapted from Bach's *Sonata No. 2 for Flute and Harpsichord.*

Rhythm Workouts

Clap and count each rhythm pattern 3 times each day.

Note: Workouts 2 and 3 look different but sound alike.

The Entertainer

CD 33/34 GM 17

Scott Joplin (1868–1917)
(adapted)

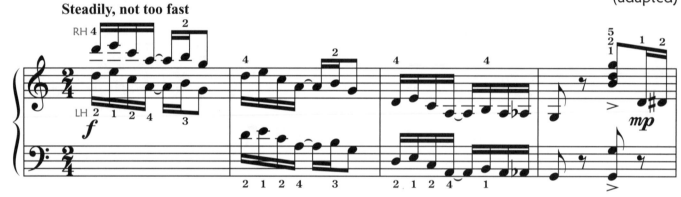

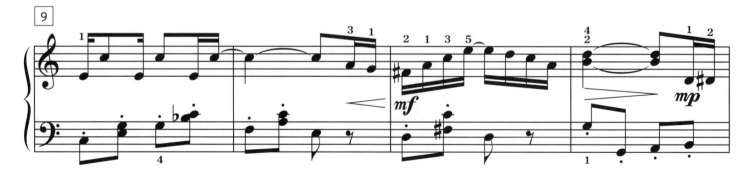

Theory Book: page 32
Performance Book: pages 38–39

Festival fantastico

CD 35/36 GM 18

Premier Performer

Exaggerate all dynamics and articulation in this piece to achieve "sparkle" and excitement.

Alfred's
Premier Performer
Piano Achievement Award

presented to

_____

Student

Congratulations!

Having successfully completed

Alfred's Premier Piano Course,

you are now a Premier Pianist.

_____   _____

Teacher   *Date*